D1555815

SPIRIT OF
LIVERPOOL

PAUL MCMULLIN

First published in Great Britain in 2014

British Library Cataloguing-in-Publication Data
A CIP record for this title is available from the British Library

ISBN 978 0 85710 090 0

PiXZ Books
Halsgrove House, Ryelands Business Park,
Bagley Road, Wellington, Somerset TA21 9PZ
Tel: 01823 653777
Fax: 01823 216796
email: sales@halsgrove.com

An imprint of Halstar Ltd, part of the Halsgrove group
of companies. Information on all Halsgrove titles
is available at: www.halsgrove.com

Printed and bound in China by Toppan Leefung

Introduction

People the world over know the city of Liverpool.

Is it because it is the birth place of the Beatles, it has two cathedrals, it has an iconic waterfront (which by the way is a World Heritage Site) or is it because it has two Premier League Football teams? Who is to say? It has shopping centres, theatres, art galleries and two world class museums.

Buildings. The city has fantastic buildings, everywhere. Around every corner – the Three Graces, the Albert Dock, Albion House, Century Building, the Philharmonic, Victoria Building, The Bridewell, The Town Hall, Stanley Dock to name just a few and not forgetting the Victorian terraced streets on the outskirts of the City Centre. All of these and much much more go to make up the city of Liverpool.

People. You don't get a city without the people – lots of famous people originated from here, some have stayed, some have left, and some have even said they won't come back! However what makes a worldwide city is the ordinary person. Liverpudlians are welcoming, humorous, self-depreciating and above all proud of their city.

Enjoy this 'little' glimpse of the city. Use it to explore further, get into its heart and be rewarded.

Paul McMullin
(www.paulmcmullin.com)

A trip on one of the Mersey ferries is a worthwhile journey; the view of the Liverpool Waterfront is always impressive at any time of day.

An unusual rear view of the Port of Liverpool building with a ferry heading towards the landing stage.

On the left, the Cunard Building and, behind the equestrian statue of King Edward VII, the Port of Liverpool Building.

RMS *Queen Mary II* is a regular visitor to the Mersey. In 2015 the three Queens, *Queen Victoria*, *Mary* and *Elizabeth* will visit Liverpool at the same time.

Opposite: the Liverpool Cruise Terminal situated at the Pier Head.

The view from the Wirral showing the whole of the Liverpool Waterfront.
Wirral residents always say that they have the best view of Liverpool.

The view from the Matau Restaurant roof terrace towards the Museum of Liverpool and the Mann Island development. The canal link from the North Docks into the Albert Dock complex and beyond in the foreground.

The Three Graces from right to left: the Port of Liverpool Building, the Cunard Building and the Royal Liver Building.

The Pier Head ferry terminal includes a restaurant, gift shop and Beatles exhibition. Beetham Tower is in the distance.

A view from across the Mersey of the *Royal Iris ferry*, the ferry terminal and the Port of Liverpool Building. St George's ventilation tower can be seen on the left.

A detail of the intricate carvings that can be seen on the Cunard Building refurbished in 2012.

The Museum of Liverpool completed in 2010 and opened to the general public in 2012.

Exhibits in the museum include a restored Liverpool Overhead Railway motor coach of 1892 and the original *Lion* steam locomotive from 1837.

The northern end of the Albert Dock complex has the Maritime Museum and the Tate Gallery. In the foreground is the Pump House which is now a pub and restaurant.

Looking over the south side of Albert Dock towards the Echo Arena and BT Convention Centre with the Liverpool Eye which is now a permanent attraction. The Beatles Story Exhibition, shops and hotels can be found here.

Looking back across Canning half tide dock towards the Hilton Hotel and Liverpool One.

The Strand, looking north. In the centre of the picture stands Albion House built in 1898, the once head office of the famous White Star Line, the owners of RMS *Titanic*.

The Strand in the opposite direction. Left to right: the Atlantic Tower Hotel, St Nicholas Tower, Wellington Buildings, the Mersey Travel head office, St George's Ventilation Tower, the Royal Liver Building.

Situated in the basement of Derby House part of Exchange Buildings is the Western Approaches Command HQ restored to how it was in 1941.

The view from India Building towards the waterfront.

Opposite: looking down Water Street past the front of the Town Hall and Martins Bank Building to the Royal Liver Building.

Minerva or Britannia? Modern thinking favours the latter. She sits atop the Town Hall and has been there since 1802.

Opposite: the rear of the Town Hall which is known as Exchange Flags with the memorial to Admiral Nelson's four victories.

The Hard Day's Night Hotel was opened in 2008 and was developed from the former Central Building built in 1884.

Opposite: an aerial view of Chavasse Park, Liverpool One and the Hilton Hotel.

Chavasse Park on a summer's day is a perfect meeting place.

Opposite: another high level view of Chavasse Park and the Liverpool One shopping area from the Hilton Hotel looking into the city.

The Walker Art Gallery.

As well as extensive galleries of paintings, the Walker also has a large collection of marble sculpture.

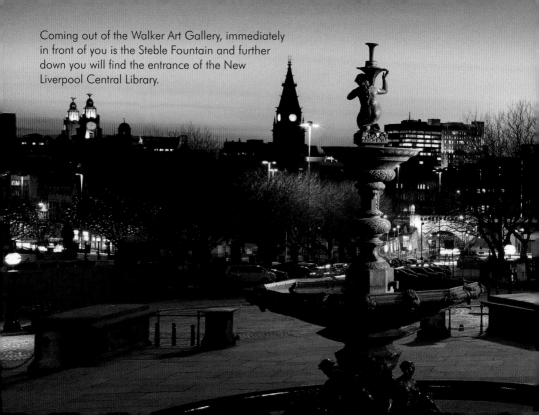

Coming out of the Walker Art Gallery, immediately in front of you is the Steble Fountain and further down you will find the entrance of the New Liverpool Central Library.

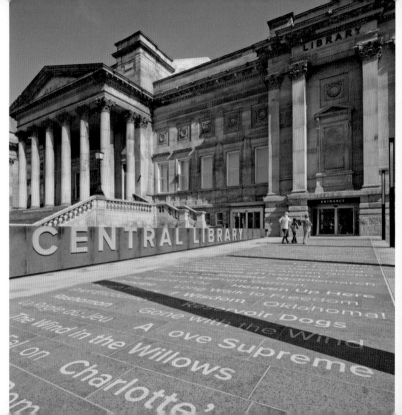

Designed by local architects Austin Smith Lord the Central Library has become a tourist attraction in its own right.

The impressive
atrium of the
new library.

St George's Hall. Completed 1839. Part of this imposing building was once an assize court were many high profile crimes were tried.

The main Ball Room has a most ornate Minton tiled floor which at various times in the year is uncovered for display.

The Wellington Column
erected in 1887.

Opposite: at the rear of
St George's Hall is a
very pleasant public
garden, known as
St John's Gardens.

Opposite: Lime Street Station. The approach was extensively remodelled in 2010. The building just to the left is the old North Western Hotel now refurbished and used for accommodation for students from Liverpool John Moores University (LJMU).

Inside Lime Street Station on the concourse are two statues commemorating two of Liverpool's finest. The politician Bessie Braddock and comedian Ken Dodd.

Liverpool has two cathedrals. The Anglican (near) and the Roman Catholic Metropolitan Cathedral also known as 'Paddy's Wigwam' for obvious reasons.

The Anglican Cathedral sits on a sandstone outcrop (St James' Mount) and dominates the skyline. The building was only finished in 1978 though construction started in 1904.

49

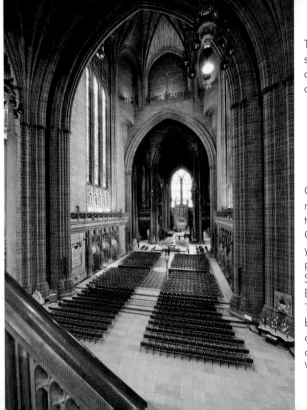

The interior is a vast open space; seating arrangements can be adjusted to suit the occasion.

Opposite: it is possible by means of lifts and stairways to visit the very top of the Cathedral. On clear days you can see beyond the Wirral peninsula to North Wales and Snowdonia and also beyond Blackpool to the Lake District. This closer view shows the beautiful Georgian houses of Gambia Terrace, in the distance you can see Liverpool Woman's Hospital.

Opposite: an aerial view of the Metropolitan Cathedral of Christ the King surrounded by numerous University buildings. The Cathedral was started in 1962 and consecrated in 1967.

The interior reflects the exterior design and can hold up to 2000 people in a circular pattern.

Leaving the Cathedral by its front entrance you look down Hope Street and past the newly refurbished Everyman Theatre you come to the Philharmonic Dining Rooms. The bar is ornately decorated in mahogany, marble and glass and this is extended into the gentleman's 'Rest Room'. Just across the Street you will find the Philharmonic Hall.

Hope Street links the two cathedrals and here are a number of art installations. The Hope Street 'Suitcases', installed by John King in 1998, just next to LIPA (Liverpool Institute of Performing Art). The labelled suitcases 'belong' to many of Hope Street Quarter's most illustrious names and organisations.

Opposite: the church of St Luke remains as a memorial to the Liverpool Blitz of 1941.

The Chinese Arch. The local China town is one of the oldest Chinese communities in the country.

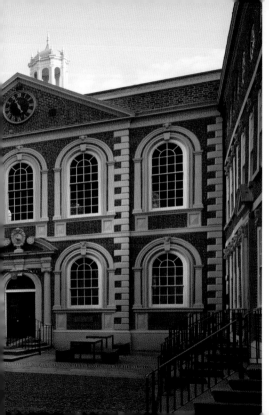

The Bluecoat (formerly the Bluecoat School) is now an Arts venue and eating place.

It's possible to relax in the exterior courtyard of the Bluecoat just a stone's throw away from the bustling Liverpool One shopping streets.

Opposite: the pedestrianised intersection of Church Street, Paradise Street and Lord Street and Whitechapel.

The iconic Waterfront as seen from a couple of miles upriver. Three centuries of development can be seen in this image.

The sun sets behind St Nicholas's church which, in the eighteenth century, used to stand directly on the waterfront of the city of Liverpool.

Liverpool One was designed to give tantalising views of important land-marks down the pedestrian streets.